CHESS

CONTENTS

	Page
The Game	2
The Moves	4
The King	4
The Pawns	4
Rooks or Castles	4
Bishops	5
The Queen	5
Knights	5
Special Moves	6
Taking Procedure (pawns) ...	6
Promotion of Pawns	7
En Passant	7
Castling	8
Check	8
Other Game Endings	11
Rules of Play	14

	Page
Notation	15
General Strategy	18
Opening Moves	19
The Middle Game	23
The End Game	29
The Cordon	30
The Opposition	30
Self-Supporting Pawns	31
King and Pawn against King ...	32
King and Pawn v. King and Piece ...	34
King, Rook and Pawn Endings ...	36
Game Openings	38
King's Pawn Openings	38
Queen's Pawn Openings	39
Conclusion	39
Problems	40

Printed in Great Britain by John S. Speight Ltd., Yeadon Yorkshire.

FOREWORD

The chief aim of this book is to increase the number of people who love the game of Chess. Previous editions have played an important part in producing more young players than we have ever had before. This is well illustrated by the large number of Junior players who compete in the Easter Congresses both on Merseyside and elsewhere throughout the Country, reaching a total well in excess of 2,000. In addition the "Sunday Times National Schools Tournament" attracts a great number of entrants, so that the numbers now taking part in this event are over 4,000.

Every year sees more and more emphasis on events for younger players, so that they now have considerably wider opportunities for playing competitive chess than ever before.

As publishers of this book, Educational Productions Ltd. deserve our warmest congratulations on the continued success that this book has achieved, and I feel certain that it will continue to make a major contribution to the encouragement of Chess in the next generation.

Sir Frederick Hoare, Bart.,

President,

The British Chess Federation

THE GAME

The chess beginner must first of all learn the names of the different chessmen, how they are arranged on the board, and what the object of the game is.

Chess is played on a board with sixty-four squares coloured alternately light and dark, and the board is always placed between the players so that each has a light-coloured square at his right-hand corner. The horizontal rows of squares are called "ranks" and the vertical rows are called "files".

A chess set consists of two similar teams of sixteen "men", one light coloured, known as White, and the other dark coloured, known as Black. In many sets, especially old ivory ones, the men are red and white, but the red men are always referred to as black.

At the start of the game the men are placed on the board as shown in Fig. 1. Notice that the White Queen faces Black Queen, White King faces Black King, etc. The player using the white set is always called "White" and his opponent "Black". "White" always starts the game and in all diagrams White moves from the bottom of the board and Black moves from the top.

The term "man" is used to refer to any of those on the board, including the pawns, but the term "piece" refers to any of the men other than the pawns. Both players have teams as shown below:—

8 Pawns—The pawns are known from the piece in front of which they stand, i.e., "Queen's pawn", "Queen's Rook's pawn", etc.

2 Rooks or Castles—Usually called Rooks.

2 Knights.   2 Bishops.   One Queen.   One King.

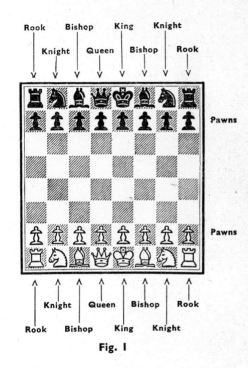

Fig. I

THE MOVES

The men can be moved on the board in various ways: but no man may move on to a square already occupied by a man of his own colour. When a man is moved to a square occupied by one of the opposing men, the latter is "taken" i.e., removed from the board and out of play.

The Pawns

These move straight up the files on which they stand, only one square at a time, except on their first move, when each pawn has the option of moving forward two squares. This only applies to each pawn's first move, and if he does not move up two squares on the first move he forfeits the option and cannot move two squares on a subsequent move.

 **KING**

  PAWN

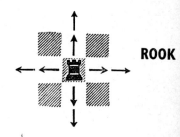 **ROOK**

The King

This is the key piece of the game because the aim is to force the opponent's King into the position where he can neither move nor remain without being taken. He is then said to be checkmated and the game is won.

The King can move in any direction, but he can only move one square at a time, and the move must not place him in a position where he is threatened with capture by another man. He is the only man on the board which is never "taken", but if he stands in such a position that he could be "taken" at the next move, he is said to be "in check" (see page 8).

Rooks or Castles

These move over as many squares as the player requires on the ranks or files, i.e. forwards, backwards or sideways. They may not be moved diagonally. The movement is limited only by the intervening presence of another man on the particular rank or file. If the man is of the same colour, i.e., friendly, the moving Rook can only advance as far as the square before that on which the friendly man stands. If the other man is of the different colour, i.e., hostile, the moving man may occupy his square and "take" him.

Bishops

BISHOP

These may be moved as far as required, but only on the diagonal, and the move is limited by the presence of other men as in the case of Rooks. Each player has two Bishops. One starts on a white square and therefore moves diagonally on to white squares only and the other starts and moves on to black squares only.

KNIGHT

QUEEN

The Queen

The Queen can be moved forwards, backwards, sideways as can a Rook, and also diagonally as can a Bishop. She can, therefore, be moved as far as required in any direction, and is thus the most powerful piece on the board, owing to her greater mobility. The move is limited by the presence of other men, as in the case of Rooks and Bishops.

Knights

These are the only men allowed to pass over other men, whether friendly or hostile. They can be moved two squares forwards, backwards or sideways (but not diagonally), then one square at right angles to this first move. The move is only limited by the presence of a friendly man on the final square of the required move, but not by the presence of any men on the intervening squares. A hostile man on the final square can be "taken".

Thus the Queen, Rooks and Bishops have a range of movement which can be varied as the play requires, whereas the King, Knights and Pawns have a fixed move. The Knights, however, cannot be blocked by the presence of other men in their path as can the others.

SPECIAL MOVES

Taking procedure (pawns)

Though the pawn may only move straight up one
square at a time, he may "take" one square forward
diagonally.

Thus in Fig. 2 the pawns block each other's path,
and neither can advance further. In Fig. 2a the white
pawn, having the move, can advance by taking the
black pawn shown ringed. If, in this position, the black
pawn had the move, the ringed pawn could either take
the white pawn or advance one square along its own
file.

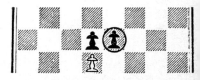

Fig. 2

Pawns block each other's path

Fig. 2a

Ringed pawn can take White pawn

Promotion of pawns

If a player succeeds in advancing a pawn to the eighth rank, i.e. on to one of the squares in the opposing first rank, he must be promoted. This is done by exchanging him for any piece except a King, for a Queen, Rook, Bishop or Knight. When promoting a pawn no regard need be taken of the number of Queens, Rooks, Bishops or Knights already on the board. It is usual to promote the pawn to be Queen as this is the most mobile piece, and a player may then have two or more Queens on the board at the same time. The promotion takes place as part of the move which takes the pawn to the eighth rank.

En Passant

When a pawn stands on his fifth rank and the opponent moves either of the two pawns on the adjacent ranks forward by two squares, as he has the option of doing in a pawn's first move, the pawn on the fifth rank may, on the next move only, move diagonally forward on to the square over which the opposing pawn has passed, and "take" that pawn. This is known as taking "en passant" or "in passing". The move is only permissible by a pawn to a pawn, and only on the next consecutive move. Figs. 3 and 3a show the position before and after Black has moved, and Fig 3b shows the position after White has taken "en passant".

Fig. 3

'En passant.'   Before Black moves

Fig. 3a

'En passant.'   After Black moves

Fig. 3b

White has taken 'en passant'

Fig. 5 Before castling
  ,, **5a** Castling to the right
  ,, **5b** Castling to the left

Castling

This is a special move allowed to the King only once in a game, and is the only time a King is moved more than one square at a time. The move, which can only be made when the intervening squares between the King and Rook are not occupied, consists in moving the King two Squares to one side and then as part of the same move, placing the Rook towards which he moves, on the far side of him. This can be done provided:—

1. That the squares between the King and required Rook are not occupied.
2. That neither the King nor required Rook has been moved previously during the game.
3. That the King is not in Check at the time of Castling, that he is not in check at the completion of Castling, and that he is not in check on the square over which he passes during Castling. A definition of "check" follows. Fig. 5 shows the position before Castling, and Figs. 5a and 5b the position after Castling to either flank.

CHECK

The King can never be taken, but if he stands in such a position that he is threatened with capture at the opponent's next move, he is said to be "in check". The King must not be left in check, so a player whose King is in check must do one of three things at his next move to release this King:

1. Move the King on to a square where he is out of check.
2. "Take" the checking piece or pawn.
3. Intervene another man so as to shield the King.

If he is unable to do any of these three things he is said to be "checkmated" and the game is ended.

In connection with point 1 above, since the King must not be moved into check, he must not be moved on to a square next to that occupied by the opposing King because he would then be in check from that piece.

In connection with point 2 above, the King may take the checking piece if it is on a square next to that on which he stands, but he must not be in check from another piece when that capture is completed.

In connection with point 3 above, if the checking piece is a Knight, it is impossible to intervene a man because the Knight can pass over the intervening man and so would still have the King in check. In this instance, only 1 and 2 can be applied.

Fig. 6

Black King is in check from White Bishop

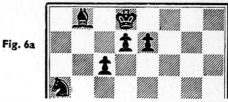

Fig. 6a

Check relieved by Knight taking Checking Bishop

Fig. 6b

Check relieved by King being moved

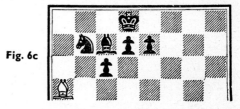

Fig. 6c

Check relieved by intervention of Black Bishop

CHECK (Continued)

Fig. 7, 7a and 7b show three simple positions of checkmate, but there are obviously an infinite variety of checkmating positions.

In Fig. 7, although the King can move one square in any direction he will still be in check by the Rook on the 8th rank if he moves on to square **a** or **e**, and by the Rook on the 7th rank if he moves on to square **b, c** or **d.**

In Fig. 7a, the Black King is in check by the Queen and will still be in check by the Queen if he moves to square **a, b, c** or **d.** If he takes the Queen he will then be in check by White King.

In Fig. 7b the Black King is still in check by the Rook if he moves to squares **a** or **e,** and by the White King if he moves to **b, c** or **d.**

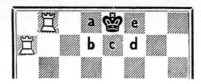

Fig. 7

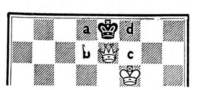

Fig. 7a

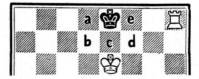

Fig. 7b

Fig. 7c

Fig. 7c shows a special variety of checkmate known as a "smothered" mate since the escape of the Black King is impeded, not by the White pieces, but by his own men. He is in check by the White Knight which can pass over the intervening Black Bishop and Queen.

Thus it will be seen that the completion of a game of chess is not dependent on the number of pieces taken, but on the attainment of a position of checkmate. However a superiority of pieces usually makes a victory more certain in the long run.

OTHER GAME ENDINGS

A game does not always end with a checkmate and a player whose chances of escaping defeat are clearly hopeless may avoid loss of time by "resigning", i.e. conceding the game to his opponent unfinished.

In addition, a game can end in a draw, as follows:
(a) The most common kind of draw is reached when the position is of such tactical equality that both players agree to a draw since they know from experience that a win cannot be obtained.

(b) Another way of reaching a draw is for the pieces to be eliminated to a point where a checkmate is no longer technically possible with those that remain on the board. Figs. 8, 8a, 8b and 8c show such positions.

Fig. 8a

Fig. 8b

Fig. 8

Fig. 8c

(c) Another form of drawn position is that known as a "Stalemate", i.e. when the opposing King is not in check and the opponent is unable to make any legal move either with his King or any other man. Figs. 9 and 9a, show two examples of a stalemate.

Note: It is possible to force a win against a King with a King and two Bishops or a King, Knight and Bishop, but not with a King and two Knights (unless the opponent plays incorrectly).

(d) The game is drawn if a player can show that 50 consecutive moves have been made without a piece being taken or a pawn moved.

(e) Another type of draw is a draw by "perpetual check", when one player can show that he can submit his opponent to an endless series of checks.

(f) A game can be drawn if one player can show that exactly the same position has recurred three times during the game. The most usual example of this type of draw is when the same move is made three times consecutively.

Fig. 9

Fig. 9a

Fig. 9b

In Fig. 9(b) Black has a winning advantage of material (i.e., a Rook to the good) and threatens checkmate, but White is able to get into a "perpetual" position.

Fig. 9(c) With black to move shows an actual finish of an international game. In this, it is interesting to note that Black can afford to offer his Rook, a piece which White dare not take for fear of being mated two moves later.

In both examples therefore, it is clear that the check can continue for ever, but after the third repetition of a similar position, a draw can be obtained on that ground, in the unlikely event of the opponent refusing to admit that the check is perpetual.

Fig. 9c

RULES OF PLAY

Before the beginner starts his first game he must learn some of the more important rules of play. The following is not, by any means a list of all the rules, but the essential points for a beginner are covered.

1. A move consists of picking up a man and transferring it to another square. The move is not completed until the player has removed his hand from the man he is moving.

2. A man that has been touched must be moved. If the player changes his mind about the move before completing the move, he may make an alternative move, but it must be with the man already touched.

3. If a player touches more than one of his own men the opponent may decide which of the touched men are to be moved, providing that a legal move is possible with that man.

4. If a player touches one of his opponent's pieces, he must take it if possible.

5. If a player touches one of his own men and one of his opponent's, he must take the opponent's man with his own "touched" man if possible. If not, the opponent must say whether he wishes his touched man to be taken or the player's touched man to be moved.

6. Once a move has been completed it cannot be retracted. That means that the player cannot change his mind and make a different move in its place.

7. A player may at any time arrange his men on the board but he must tell his opponent before he does so. He may also ask his opponent to arrange his own pieces but he must not touch or arrange his opponent's men.

8. If an illegal move is made and discovered later in the game, the men must be set out in the positions they had before the illegal move and the game continued with a legal move using the man used for the illegal move. If the positions before the illegal move cannot be decided, the game must be discontinued and is void.

9. If a penalty cannot legally be complied with, a further penalty is not enforced.

10. If an opponent claims an illegal move as a penalty, he thereby forfeits his right to exact a penalty for the offence in question.

11. Castling may not be enforced as a penalty move.

12. The players must not comment on any moves while the game is in progress, nor may they consult any written notes which bear upon the game being played.

13. Players must not seek advice or information from onlookers while the game is in progress.

NOTATION

The beginner is now ready to start playing and he will need some guidance on elementary tactics and strategy. Reference must be made to particular moves on the board, so it is necessary to understand how chess moves are recorded on paper.

There are two main systems of notation:—
1. The British or Descriptive System.
2. The Continental or Algebraic System.

The British System.

Although the British system is much more cumbersome than the Continental system, it is used in almost all British books and articles on chess.

The Bishops, Knights and Rooks on the King's side are known as King's Bishop, King's Knight and King's Rook and those on the Queen's side are known as Queen's Bishop, Queen's Knight and Queen's Rook.

The files are known by the name of the pieces standing on them at the start of the game.

The squares are numbered 1 — 8 along the files from each end, and each square is referred to by the file name and square number, e.g., King's Bishop 1.

It will be seen that White King's Bishop 1 is the same as Black King's Bishop 8, etc. and Fig 10a shows the board with the square names marked from the point of view of White with the notation for Black put in upside down.

The pawns are known by the names of their files, i.e., King's Rook's pawn, or Queen's Knight's pawn, etc.

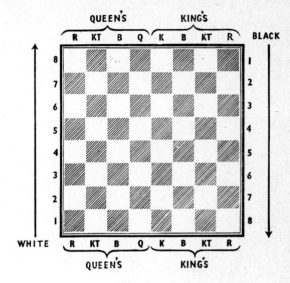

Fig. 10

The standard abbreviations are:

King ... K   King's Bishop ... KB   King's Knight ... K Kt
Queen ... Q   Queen's Bishop ... QB   Queen's Knight ... Q Kt
Pawn ... P

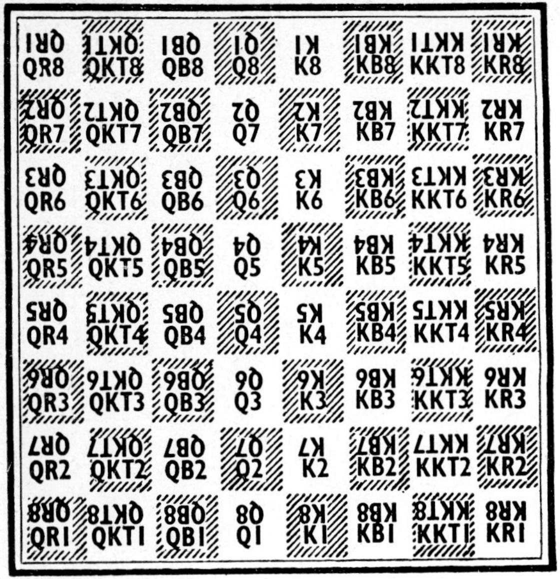

Fig. 10a

It will be clearly seen from Figs. 10 and 10a, how the different squares are named for the purpose of recording the various moves.

The moves in the game are numbered consecutively, and White always starts the game. If White, as his first move, advances his King's pawn by two squares, the notation is 1. P — K4, indicating that the pawn on the King's file has been advanced to the fourth rank. If Black replies by a similar advance of his King's pawn it is recorded 1. P — K4. If then White advances his King's Knight two squares up the file and one square at right angles on to the Bishop's file the notation is 2. Kt -- KB3 (correct also is KKt — B3), and if Black protects his now menaced King's pawn by a similar movement of his Queen's Knight the record is 2. Kt. — QB3 (or QKt — B3).

The complete record would read:—

    1. P — K4, P — K4
    2. Kt — KB3, Kt — QB3

A special notation is used to record Castling:—

    0 — 0 indicates Castles King's Side
    0 — 0 — 0 indicates Castles Queen's Side

The notation x is used to record a piece taken e.g. B x B means Bishop takes Bishop.

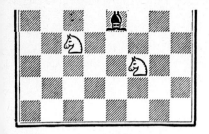

Fig. II Record must indicate which Knight takes the Black Bishop

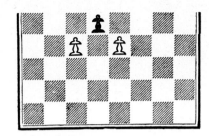

Fig. IIa KP × P or BP × P

Fig. IIb B × P

If more than one similar piece can make the required move the record must clearly show which one is to be moved.

Thus in Fig. 11 it can be seen that either Knight can take the Black Bishop, and the record would read Kt (B3) x B, or Kt (B4) x B according to which Knight has to make the capture.

Similarly in Fig. 11a the move to take the Black pawn must be recorded KP x P or BP x P, according to which pawn makes the capture.

If a move leaves the opposing King in check, the notation (ch) is put after the record of the move, i.e. B — Kt 5 ch. Fig. 11b shows a well-known position of the men on the board. The White Bishop has the choice of taking one of two Black pawns. It is not necessary to indicate which of two pawns is to be taken, because the record B x P refers only to the Black Bishop's pawn because, if the Rook's pawn is to be taken, the record would be B x P ch., since the Black King would be in check when the move was completed.

GENERAL STRATEGY

The beginner is now able to set out his board and men, knows the permissible moves, can record his moves, and has a knowledge of the basic rules of the game and its object. Now he can consider some of the principles of elementary strategy and tactics.

A game of chess must always be governed by a definite scheme, or series of schemes, all moving in accordance with a general strategical plan, but modified from time to time to meet immediate tactical necessities. With inexperienced players, the general scheme is likely to be more or less hazy, or even non-existent, and the game may develop more or less accidentally from a series of problems and tactical threats dealt with move by move.

This need not worry the beginner, because every game he plays will widen his experience, especially if played against a stronger opponent, until he has gained a reasonable grasp of general tactics. It is of vital importance throughout that no move should be made without a reason. The move may be wrong because the reason is wrong, but practice, tuition and experience will correct the reasoning in due course. It is absolutely essential that every move be made for a definite purpose. Aimless chess is invariably bad chess and losing chess.

The aim of every player is to checkmate his opponent, but since the players start the game each with the same number of men in the same positions, it is obvious that several moves must be made before a direct attack can be attempted on the hostile King. It is necessary therefore for the beginner to concentrate first on gaining positional advantages which may lead to material ones at a later stage.

The basic strategical principle generally adopted is to try to gain control of the centre, i.e., of the squares K4, K5, Q4 and Q5 and those adjacent to them. The opening moves should be developed so that an advantage is gained from mutual co-operation, by a central control in attack, and not, of course, at the same time overlooking the defensive front.

If such a control can be succesfully established a winning continuation will usually be forthcoming provided that the player can find it. The reason for trying to gain central control is that the men have then the greatest mobility for use on all parts of the board. Concentration on one flank tends to have the disadvantage that the opponent will probably take counter-measures on the opposite flank. Often one player is attacking on one flank while the other is launching a counter-attack on the other side without bothering to concentrate on defensive measures at the threatened spot, and the victory goes to the player whose attack gets home first.

Control is a word frequently used when describing chess tactics. A square is said to be controlled by a player when he has more pieces bearing on it than his opponent has. Therefore a square need not be occupied to be controlled, and, in fact, a square is not controlled, although occupied, unless the occupying man is adequately defended by at least as many men as there are hostile men attacking it.

From this definition it can be seen that there are two methods of attaining central control, the first by advancing pawns into the centre and maintaining them by adequate support, and the second by reserving an initial pawn advance by bringing the longer-ranged pieces such as the Knights and Bishops to bear on the centre squares from a distance. In this second case an eventual central pawn advance will have to be made but the strategical idea is that, whereas an immediate advance commits a player to a definite course of action, the reservation of such an advance leaves the opponent without such a clear-cut tactical problem for solution.

In practice, however, it is usually found that White prefers to exploit his advantage of the first move by an immediate pawn advance into the centre. In former years Black invariably met such an advance with a similar reply so as to maintain a 50% control of the centre by symmetry of moves, but to-day the reservation of the central pawn advance is also frequently used. Thus the move 1. P—Q4 is often met by 1. Kt—KB3, and 1. P—K4 by 1. P—QB4, in each case contesting the advance of a second pawn in the centre by White but reserving the advance of either of the Black central pawns.

OPENING MOVES

Having considered the basic strategical ideas of the start of a chess game, we must now consider the immediate tactical problems likely to be met in trying to put them into effect. If both players rush aimlessly into the centre, there will be some sort of general exchange leading to an eventual draw. It is therefore necessary to manoeuvre with a view to making moves which will leave the opponent's pieces in bad positions. or possibly to offer the sacrifice of a pawn or even a piece in order to obtain a better position if the sacrifice is accepted.

Fig. 12 Greek Bishop

Fig. 13 King's Gambit

Fig. 13a Queen's Gambit

For example, one well known move which achieves this is called the "Greek Bishop". In this series of moves, the Bishop is placed so it can take the King's Rook pawn while at the same time there is no opposing Knight on the opponent's square KB3. In Fig. 12 play with White to move, would go:—

1. B x P ch., K x B.
2. Kt — Kt5 ch., K — Kt1.
3. Q — R5.

and wins since Black has no adequate defence against the threat of the fourth move Q — R7 check mate. It is, of course, open to Black to decline the sacrifice by playing 1. K — R1, but if he does he will lose a pawn and his King will be dangerously exposed. He can

also play 2. K — Kt3, but then his King will not escape disaster for more than a few moves in such an open unprotected position.

Pawn sacrifices can occur at any time in the game, but they are most frequently found early on in the game in a gambit theme. In this a pawn, known as the gambit pawn, is sacrificed with the idea thereby of decreasing the opponent's ability to fight for the control of the central squares.

The gambit pawn is usually on one of the Bishop's files so that, if the offer is accepted, one of the opposing pawns is drawn off the central files. If the gambit is offered in the opening stages it is known as the King's Gambit or the Queen's Gambit, according to whether the King's or Queen's Bishop's pawn is sacrificed.

The opening moves of the King's and Queen's gambits respectively are:—

| 1. | P — K4, P — K4 | | 1. | P — Q4. P — Q4 |
| 2. | P — KB4 | and | 2. | P — QB4 |

as shown in Figs. 13 and 13a.

In the Victorian and Edwardian eras these gambit attacks proved very dangerous and led to some extremely brilliant games, owing to the fact that Black invariably tried to hold his pawn advantage. For this reason it later became more customary for players to decline gambits when offered. Modern analysis, however, has shown that the correct treatment of gambits is to accept the gambit pawn and then to concentrate on reaching positional equality without trying to hold the extra pawn. If this course is followed Black can achieve equality of position with little trouble, and to such an extent has this proved to be the case that gambit openings, with the exception of the Queen's Gambit, are rarely found in first-class chess to-day because they offer too safe a drawing chance to the second player.

The **Queen's Gambit** can be accepted or declined with equal success provided that Black plays his game accurately, but it is being played less to-day because the answer to 1. P — Q4 is far more often 1. Kt — KB3 than 1. P — Q4, following the theory of a delayed central pawn advance. In such cases it is not possible to offer the Queen's Bishop's pawn as a gambit.

In gambits based on the opening 1. P — K4 the basic principles for Black are:—

1. To accept the gambit pawn.

2. To concentrate on a development which combats the control of the centre, and to return the gambit pawn in the course of play, unless White by incorrect moves allows him to retain his pawn advantage safely.

3. To play ... P — Q4 successfully as soon as possible.

Once Black has achieved the last-named objective, he has gained equality of position, but it must be emphasised that he must be able to play ... P — Q4 **successfully.** To play this move in the face of an already established control is merely suicidal.

Typical opening moves against the **King's Gambit** used to be:—

1. P — K4, P — K4
2. P — KB4, P x P
3. Kt — KB3, P — KKt4

Here Black is trying to hold his pawn advantage, and it is against such attempts that this opening can be so dangerous. The more modern continuation would probably be:—

1. P — K4, P — K4
2. P — KB4, P x P
3. Kt — KB3, P — Q4
4. P x P, Kt — KB3

Here Black has returned the gambit pawn and successfully played ... P — Q4 with the result that, although he no longer has a pawn advantage, he has no disadvantage of position. In this example it would be incorrect for White to play 4. P — K5 because Black could then reply 4. ... P — KKt4 and hold his pawn advantage. This is the type of positional mistake referred to in 2. on the previous page. If in the above line of play White plays 3. B — B4 play could go:—

3.   ... P — Q4
4.   B x P, Kt — KB3
5.   Kt — QB3, B — QKt5

Finally it may be mentioned that the attractive looking move 3. ... Q — R5 ch. leads to no advantage for Black, who gains only a superficial advantage by forcing the White King to move while the Black Queen remains dangerously exposed to attack.

In the opening known as the **Danish Gambit, Black's** three basic principles expressed in the following moves can be successfully applied:—

1.   P — K4, P — K4
2.   P — Q4, P x P
3.   P — QB3, P — Q4
4.   KP x P, Q x P
5.   P x P, Kt — QB3
6.   Kt — KB3, Kt — B3
7.   Kt — B3, B — QKt5

Fig. 14

reaching the position shown in Fig. 14. Here again Black has successfully played ... P — Q4 at move 3, and in the ensuing pawn exchanges has returned the gambit pawn but gained a solid equality of position.

Notice that Black's last move protects his Queen by pinning the White Knight which cannot move without disclosing a check. Such pins play a great part in the tactics of chess.

Against openings 1. P — K4, the struggle for central control is usually decided by whether or not Black can force the move ... P — Q4 successfully, and this applies equally to lines of play where no gambits are employed.

The examples just given of gambit play illustrate the need to plan the opening of a game of chess. Both sides try to develop their pieces as quickly as possible within the guiding limits of the strategy they have in mind. Formerly, so much emphasis was laid on speed of development that it was considered tactically wrong to make any pawn moves except those which were absolutely necessary to assist development.

The decline in gambit play in recent years has caused chess players to turn more and more towards lines of play leading to restriction of hostile development, and in such lines there are many pawn moves which can be most useful, and which are accordingly now considered quite correct. It may be thought that this idea of restriction is defensive rather than offensive and consequently undesirable, but this is not so.

During the present century, chess theory and analysis have reached a high level of intensity and accuracy, with the natural result that among reasonably strong players it is growing more and more difficult to win by the comparatively simple and direct means employed by former generations. The tendency is now rather to aim at reaching positional advantages which restrict the opponent's freedom of movement by denying him the use of certain squares. In such games pawns are of paramount importance. The offensive idea still remains behind such a plan just as in the case of a boxer who tries to manœuvre his opponent into a corner of the ring before going in to his attack.

THE MIDDLE GAME

We have considered the principles of opening play and now we must consider those underlying the game in its more advanced stages, often known as the Middle Game. The struggle for central control will have been settled one way or the other and the players will be making further plans for gaining the final objective of the game, the checkmating of the opponent.

At this stage both players will be mainly concerned with the gaining and the prevention of tactical positional advantages. It is possible that faulty play in the opening by one of the players, may present a positional weakness ready-made for exploitation, but in these days of concentrated opening analysis, it is far more probable that both sides will have developed in the early part of the game with reasonable correctness.

In such circumstances accurate planning is essential for success, and a constant search should be maintained to discover small positional advantages and also to avoid similar chances for the opponent in the player's own position. To do this, the player must correctly appreciate the existing situation in the same way as a soldier studies military tactics. Positions, strength, mobility, and objectives must be considered and a plan formed by which it is hoped to win the game. Strength in the opening stages will always be equal over the whole board, but not necessarily so in any one part of it, and these local discrepancies play a big part in the making of plans for attack or defence.

Each player should try to understand his opponent's objective as indicated by his moves, but if, after due consideration, no real reason appears to underly a specific move by the opponent, then the player should ignore it and continue with his own plans. Unrecognised, and possibly non-existent dangers, should never be allowed to deter a chess player. If there is a threat which has not been realised the player will soon learn it and his experience will be enlarged thereby.

A direct attack on the opposing King will not often be possible in the early stages of the game, but if any small weakness of position can be found in the hostile ranks, and can be successfully exploited, then the attacker can most often gain ultimate victory as a result. Thus, however attractive it may be to make direct attacks towards the hostile King, it is usually sounder strategy to locate a positional weakness, often in another part of the board, and to concentrate all available forces on exploiting it.

The most frequent weaknesses in a position occur in the pawn formations, largely owing to the fact that a pawn cannot retreat and therefore, when once moved, is committed for better or worse. The most common weakness among the pawns is what is known as a "backward pawn".

A backward pawn is one which stands on a file on which there is no hostile pawn and which cannot be defended by one of its own pawns. Such a pawn should be attacked at once with all forces possible. If it can be won, a winning position can usually be gained out of the ensuing exchanges, while if not, then at least the opponent will be compelled to tie up most of his forces in defending it.

There are other weaknesses such as a piece left unprotected or a piece pinned down, but these are usually temporary, while a pawn weakness is usually of a fixed and lasting type, and is usually most dangerous and troublesome if properly exploited. The only courses open to the player with a backward pawn are:—

1. To defend it as well as possible.

2. To force it forward to a point where it is defended by another pawn and so is no longer backward.

3. To block the file with a piece and so protect the pawn from attack.

4. To force an exchange which will compel the opponent to retake on to the file with a pawn, then the pawn will no longer be backward.

5. To abandon the pawn to its fate but to try to gain a pawn somewhere else on the board in exchange, or at any rate some compensating positional advantage.

6. To force the pawn forward so as to get rid of it by exchange.

Fig. 15

Fig. 16

Fig. 15 shows a Black Queen's pawn which is both isolated and backward. White has concentrated his attack on it and is now about to take it. He is attacking it with a Queen, two Rooks, a Knight and a Bishop, a total of five pieces, against Black's defending Queen, Rook, Knight and Bishop, a total of four pieces.

Sometimes, however, it is not necessary to win a backward pawn to win a game, because the threat to the pawn may lead the opponent to adopt a losing line to try to save it. In the position shown in Fig. 16 Black has an ingenious plan for liquidating his backward Queen's Bishop's pawn which, however, leads to a loss because he has thus left his Queen in a weak position.

Play after White's 16th move went as follows:—

White	Black
16	B x B
17 Q x B	P — QB4 (a)
18 P x P	Q — R4 (b)
19 P — QKt3 (c)	B x P
20 Kt — Kt5	P — KR3 (d)
21 Q — R7 (ch)	K — B1
22 Q — R8 (ch)	K — K2
23 Q x KtP	P x Kt
24 Q x KtP (ch)	K — Q3
25 K — K2	QR — B1
26 R — B4 (e)	K — B3
27 KR — QB1	K — Kt3 (f)
28 P — KR4 (g)	P — KB4 (h)
29 Q — Kt7	R — K2
30 Q — K5	R — B3
31 R — B4	resigns

(See overleaf for an explanation of the letters in brackets after moves 17, 18, 19, 20, 26, 27, 28.)

(a) Black has an ingenious plan for liquidating his backward pawn.

(b) The plan matures, but Black has in the process moved his Queen out of the game.

(c) White cannot give up his QRP because of Black's subsequent deadly wing pawn attack.

(d) Another ingenious move. Black thinks he can get his King to safety on the Queen's wing if White attacks, and such an attack must cost White his Knight. White, however, is prepared to sacrifice.

(e) Preparing for the deadly 27 R — Q1 ch. and winning. Black sees this and moves before he is driven.

(f) The Black Queen now has no move.

(g) White KRP can now advance unopposed.

(h) A better defence would be R — B2; then 29, P — R5, R(1) — QB1; 30, P — R6 B — Q3; 31, Q x Q, K x Q; 32, R x R, B x R; 33, P — R7 R — KR1.

Another example of weakness in the pawn-formation is that of "holes" or "fore-posts" which may be occupied successfully by an opposing piece. The definition of a fore-post is that it should be a square which cannot be attacked by an opposing pawn.

Fig. 17

Foreposts are most commonly created on the fifth rank by the advance of the opposing pawns to their fourth rank. They are known as "contingent" or "absolute" if occupied by a minor piece, i.e., a Knight or Bishop, according to whether the occupying piece can or cannot be attacked by an opposing minor piece. Fig. 17 gives an example of an absolute forepost.

If the Black Bishop stood on K2 instead of KB2 the fore-post would be contingent. It will be noted that White has an alternative fore-post on his square K5.

As a general rule it is most profitable to occupy an available fore-post with a Knight, and there are occasions when it will be sound play to accept a losing exchange, i.e., to give up a major piece for a minor in order to get a Knight on to the required square. (The major pieces are the Queens and Rooks).

Fig. 18 gives an example of such play, and it will be noted how the White Knight, once established, hampers the Black defence on every turn, and finally, supports a winning attack.

White	Black
1 R x B	P x R
2 Kt — Kt4	K — Kt2
3 Q — B3	R — KB1
4 Kt — B6 (*a*)	Q — B3
5 P — KR4	R — R2
6 R — KB1	Q — B1
7 Q — Kt4 (*b*)	Kt — B4 (*c*)
8 R — B3	QR — KB2 (*d*)
9 Q x P (ch) (*e*)	K — R1
10 B x Kt	resigns (*f*)

(*a*) Now the Knight stands firm on his fore-post, dominating all Black's efforts.

(*b*) Threatening 8. B x P, Kt x B   9. P — R5 winning.

Fig. 18

(*c*) A clever effort to shut out the threat of the White Bishop and to bring his Queen's Rook into action.

(*d*) This move, which seems to get Black out of trouble, is actually suicide.

(*e*) If 9 ... K x Q, 10. R — Kt3 mate.

(*f*) There is no reply to Q x P (ch).

Another usual weakness in the pawn formation is made by the movement of the pawns in front of a Castled King. Although such moves sometimes have to be made, they should never be made unless absolutely forced since a potential weakness is always left which the opponent may be able to exploit later in the game if not immediately.

Fig. 19

Fig. 19 shows a position in which Black has played ... P — KR3 at some earlier stage in the game, with the result that now White is able to sacrifice a Rook, thereby gaining a winning attack.

Play, after Black's 22nd move went as follows:—

23 R x KRP	P x R
24 Q — Kt6 ch.	K — R1
25 Q x P ch.	K — Kt1
26 R — Q5.	

and wins since Black cannot defend the threat of checkmate by 27. R — KKt5. He can intervene with the Queen or Bishop but the Rook will simply take them and the threat remains.

Notice that after 24. Q — Kt6 (ch). Black cannot play 24 ... P x Q because this move would disclose a check from the White Bishop on QB4. In other words the pawn is pinned, another example of the value and danger of such pins.

In Fig. 20 Black moves a pawn in front of his Castled King, although he is not forced to do so by his opponent. He makes this move out of fear of attack from the White Knight which he wishes to drive away. The results are disastrous:—

1	P — KR3
2 Kt x P	R x Kt
3 Q — Kt6	Q — Q2
4 R — B3	Kt — Q4 (*a*)
5 R x R	Q x R
6 R — K8 ch.	resigns (*b*)

(*a*) If 4 ... K — B1 5. R x Kt R x R 6. Q — R7 and wins.

(*b*) If 6 ... Q x R 7. Q x Q ch and wins.

Once again it will be seen that the pin by the White Bishop plays a great part in these manœuvres.

Fig. 20

Fig. 21 Winning position for King and two Bishops

Fig. 21a Winning position for King, Bishop and Knight

Fig. 22 The Cordon (see page 30)

THE END GAME

After the above brief examples of some tactical ideas in the middle game, we examine briefly some general principles of end-game play. This part of the game is of the greatest importance, since it is possible for a good end-game player to retrieve a disadvantageous middle game, or for a good middle-game to be thrown away by poor end-game play.

All players are strongly recommended to play out their games as often as possible to a point where a justifiable resignation is possible. For novices, it is excellent practice for all games to be played right out to a checkmate without any resignations.

The field of end-game play is so vast that it is only possible to give a very brief outline of some of the more common basic types, but these will establish certain principles which can be applied to end-games in general.

It has already been stated that checkmate is possible against a solitary King by King and Queen, King and Rook, King and two Bishops, and King, Bishop and Knight.

Figs. 7, 7a and 7b have shown the checkmating position with King and Rook.

It will be seen that the play in each case is to drive the opposing King into a corner. In the case of King, Bishop and Knight, it must be a corner square of the same colour as that on which the Bishop stands. He is then pinned there with the King and Bishop restricting his move to the squares R1 and Kt1. After this the third piece is brought up to administer mate. Such end-games are, however, of mainly theoretical interest as they are rarely likely to occur in actual play.

As a general rule, most end-games tend to centre round the struggle to win by the promotion of a pawn, and they can be classed generally under the following headings:

(a) King and pawn against King.
(b) King and pawn against King and piece.
(c) King, Rook and pawn endings.

Before considering end-games in detail it is necessary to define three terms frequently used:—

1. The cordon or Queening square.
2. The opposition.
3. Self-supporting pawns.

The Cordon

This is an imaginery square on the board. One side is made up of the square on which the pawn stands and the squares up to and including its eighth rank.

The Black outline in Fig 22 shows the cordon of the pawn on KKt3, and the dotted line shows its cordon after it has advanced one square to KKt4.

The opposing King, in order to catch the pawn before it can achieve promotion, must be able to enter the cordon before the pawn moves. In Fig. 22 Black can do this if he has the move, but if White moves first then the pawn will enter the smaller cordon and cannot be caught in time.

The Opposition

A King is said to have the opposition when he is separated from the other King by an odd number of squares either on a file, rank or diagonal, and the opposing King has the move. In Fig. 23 the White King has the opposition if it is Black's turn to move, and the dotted squares indicate the other squares on the board on which the Black King could stand and the Kings still be in opposition. The gaining or avoidance of the opposition is the most important individual tactical feature of end-game play.

The tactical value of having the opposition is that the opposing King is forced to concede control of squares to his opponent when he moves, and that the latter then has the choice of moving so as to keep the opposition or of taking advantage of the territory conceded.

Fig. 24

Fig. 25 ⟶

⟵ **Fig. 23**

In the former case he would be playing for a draw, and in the latter for a win. In Fig. 24 Black can draw if he has the opposition, since he will be able to keep the opposition after each move, but if White has the opposition, i.e., Black has to move first, then White must be able to win by taking one of the Black pawns. The example is a simple one which the novice can work out for himself.

Self-Supporting Pawns

Pawns are so described when they are in a position where they cannot be attacked by the hostile King and one of them taken without the other one being able to reach the eighth rank and gain promotion. In Fig. 25 both sets of pawns are self-supporting. The case of the white pawns is clear since if Black plays 1 … K x P, White answers 2 P — R6 and the Black King cannot catch it as he is outside the cordon. The Black pawns, however, require more careful play, and the rule is that the pawns should not be moved until one of them is attacked, and then the other one should be moved. Thus play might go:—

1. K — K6   P — R4 (moving the unattacked pawn)
2. K — B5   K — Q6
3. K — B4   K — B5
4. K — Kt3   P — B4
5. K — R4   P — B5, etc.

King and Pawn against King

In endings where a King and Pawn face a King alone a win should only be gained if the King can lead his pawn on the 6th rank. If this position can be reached the pawn can be forced home whether its King has the opposition or not. The term "should" is used because it is always possible for a player to throw away a drawn position by incorrect play. In Fig. 26 White can only win if he has the move.

1.	K — Q2	K — Q2		1.	....	K — K2
2.	K — Q3	K —·K2	but	2.	K — Q2	K — K3
3.	K — K4	K — K3		3.	K — K3	K — K4
4.	P — K3 and wins				securing the opposition and drawing.	

Note:—In the first examples White can only win because he has the waiting move 4. P — K3 at his disposal. If the pawn had started on K3 the game would have been drawn as Black would have the opposition.

Fig. 27 provides an interesting study of the necessity for really careful calculation of time and distance. Play went:—

1. P — Kt5 ch., K — Kt2
2. P — R6 ch., K — Kt3
3. K — Kt4, K — B2

and a draw was agreed because White was afraid to take his King up the Board to force one of his pawns through as this would leave the Black Queen's Pawn free to advance. It is, however, possible for White to win despite the promotion of the Black pawn, e.g.:—

4.	K — B5	P — Q6	8.	K — B7	P — Q8
5.	P — Kt6 ch.	K — Kt1			(=Q)
6.	K — B6	P — Q7	9.	P — Kt7 ch.	K x RP
7.	P — R7 ch.	K — R1	10.	P — Kt8 ch.	
				(=Q)	K — R3
			11.	Q — Kt6 Mate	

Thus it will be seen that, while not complicated, these King and pawn endings offer many possibilities for error and need careful calculation and play. The main tactical points for consideration are:—

1. The calculation of distances, e.g. the cordon.

2. The correct evaluation of the need to gain or avoid the opposition.

3. The tactical implications of passed or self-supporting pawns.
   (Note: A passed pawn is one which can advance without interference from another hostile pawn).

When there are two pawns against one, having the opposition is of great value. In Fig. 28 Black cannot

Fig. 26

Fig. 27

Fig. 28

win since the White pawns are self-supporting and so cannot be attacked without one being able to reach the eighth rank. Black must, therefore, play for a draw which he can get if he has the move but not otherwise:—

   1. .... K — Q4
   2. K — B4   K — Q5 or 2. K — K3   K — K4

and Black draws by keeping the opposition indefinitely. With the move, White wins by:—

   1. K — K3   K — Q4
   2. K — Q3   K — B4
   3. K — K4   K — B3
   4. K — Q4   and wins.

Note:—It does not matter if Black plays 3 ...... K — Kt3 or B3. It should also be noted that White cannot win by an immediate advance of the QRP since the Black King is within its cordon and so can catch it, after which Black can get a draw on the lines shown in Fig. 30.

The final assessment of an end-game position depends as much on position as on number of men left. Equality of men usually means a draw, and superiority such as an extra pawn should usually enable a win to be obtained. One of the most usual positions where equality does not mean a draw is that in which there is a distant passed pawn. This is a pawn which stands

Fig. 29

Fig. 30

Fig. 30a

on the far side of the board from the main body of pawns, so that the opposing King cannot stop it taking the Queen, and at the same time protect his own pawns from attack by the other King.

In Fig. 29 it will be seen that after:—
1. P — KKt4, P x P
2. P x P

the White King's Knight's pawn is passed and distant, so that if the Black King opposes its advance, the White King can win the Black pawns and can then force a Queen on the Queen's side of the board. If the Black King goes to the defence of his own pawns, the distant Knight's pawn Queen's unopposed.

King and Pawn against King and Piece

In the King and pawn against King and piece ending, the game is usually a draw, if the piece is a minor one. This is because it is not possible to mate with a King and minor piece, and so the player with the piece merely gives it up for the pawn, leaving two Kings only on the board and a drawn game. Only in very exceptional circumstances is it possible to avoid such a sacrifice. It may be occasionally possible to Queen the pawn and win if the Knight or Bishop is hopelessly misplaced.

With regard to major pieces, the result of a King and pawn against King and Rook depends entirely on the position. It is clear that the pawn must be taken without the loss of the Rook, and the Rook alone cannot stop the advance of the King and pawn. Thus the result usually depends on the position of the Kings.

If the pawn is well forward and closely supported by its King, the game can usually be drawn, but if the opposing King is already in front of it there may still be winning chances. It is impossible to lay down a rule for such positions and each must be judged on its merits. But it can be said that a King and Rook will not necessarily win against a King and pawn.

The only other major piece is the Queen, and here the position is more definite. A King and Queen can win against a King and pawn except when the pawn has reached the seventh rank on a Bishop's or Rook's file and is supported by its King. In such a position, unless the opposing King is within reach of the square Kt3 close to the pawn, the King and pawn can draw. The principle of the win with the King and Queen is to check the King until he is driven in front of his pawn and then to take advantage of the blocking of the pawn to advance the Queen's King towards the pawn. These tactics are repeated until the King is next to the pawn and the Queen can take it without being retaken. Fig. 30 gives an example of such play:—

1. Q — K7 ch. K — B8
2. Q — Q6   K — K7
3. Q — K5 ch. K — B7
4. Q — Q4 ch. K — K7
5. Q — K4 ch. K — B7
6. Q — Q3   K — K8
7. Q — K3 ch. K — Q8
8. K — Q7   K — B7
9. Q — K2   K — B8
10. Q — B4 ch. K — Kt7
11. Q — Q3   K — B8
12. Q — B6 ch. K — Q8
13. K — Q6

and so on until the White King reaches the square Q3 and a winning position.

In the case of the exceptions mentioned, it will be seen from Fig. 30a that if the White Queen takes the pawn on KB7 the Black King will be stalemated and the game is therefore a draw as the pawn cannot be successfully taken.

King, Rook and pawn Endings

The following general statements apply to endings involving King and Rook against King, Rook and pawn:—

1. If the opposing King is in front of the pawn, a draw can be obtained.
2. If the opposing King is cut off from the pawn by two files or more he will lose, except perhaps in case of a pawn very far back.
3. If the opposing King is cut off by one file only, he can draw if he is in the smaller half of the board, but can-lose if he is in the larger.

Fig. 31 shows the King in front of the pawn and after:—

Fig. 31

1. P — K5   R — QR3
2. P — K6   R — R8

It is clear that Black can draw the game by perpetual check from behind or else he will win the pawn and secure a draw in that way.

If the King is cut off from the pawn by two files or more as in Fig 31a, the plan for White is to get his King in front of his pawn on the eighth rank and then to bring it out again so as to block the check from the Black Rook at the appropriate moment.

Fig. 31 a

1. K — B5	R — QKt3	8. R — Kt4	R — Q7
2. P — K6	R — Kt8	9. K — B7	R — B7 ch.
3. K — B6	R — B8 ch.	10. K — K6	R — K7 ch.
4. K — K7	R — K8	11. K — B6	R — B7 ch.
5. K — B7	R — B8 ch.	12. K — K5	R — K7 ch.
6. K — K8	R — K8	13. R — K4	
7. P — K7	R — Q8		and wins

Fig. 31 b

Fig 31b shows the position when the King is cut off by one file in the smaller section of the board. Black can draw this game and it is clear that after:—

1. K — Q5 R — R4 (ch.)

the game is a draw by perpetual check or the loss of the White pawn, since if the White King takes shelter on the KB file, Black immediately plays his King across in front of the pawn and secures a draw as in Fig. 31.

In Fig. 31c the King is cut off by one file in the larger half of the board and will lose after:—

1. .... R — R5 ch.
2. K — B5 R — R4 ch.
3. K — B6 R — R3 ch.
4. K — Kt5

and the White pawn must now reach K6 and eventually K8 and win.

Fig. 31 c

In many of the examples quoted, statements have been made, as in the explanation of Fig. 31c, that the White pawn must now be able to get to K8, or that White now wins. It will be excellent practice for the beginner to work out the truth of such statements for himself because they are not always obvious except to more experienced players, and in working them out, the player will gradually learn more of the game.

GAME OPENINGS

Some basic principles and examples have now been given of the start, the middle and the end of a game of chess and finally there are now given, without any comments, a few examples of some of the more usual openings used in club games. These are intended to give the beginner some sort of picture of how a game starts, but the theory of opening play is so immense that nothing more can be attempted here.

King's Pawn Openings

Ruy Lopez

1. P — K4, P — K4
2. Kt — KB3, Kt — QB3
3. B — Kt5, P — QR3
4. B — R4, P — Q3 ... or   4. ... ... Kt — B3
5. B x Kt ch., P x B   5. 0 — 0   B — K2
6. P — Q4, P — B3   6. R — K1, P — QKt4

Giuoco Piano

1. P — K4, P — K4
2. Kt. — KB3, Kt — QB3
3. B — B4, B — B4
4. P — B3, Kt — B3
5. P — Q4, P x P
6. P x P, B — Kt5 ch.

French Defence

1. P — K4, P — K3
2. P — Q4, P — Q4
3. Kt — QB3, Kt — KB3
4. B — KKt5, B — K2
5. P — K5, KKt — Q2
6. B x B, Q x B

Caro-Kann Defence

1. P — K4, P — QB3
2. P — Q4, P — Q4
3. Kt — QB3, P x P
4. Kt x P, B — B4
5. Kt — Kt3, B — Kt3

Sicilian Defence

1. P — K4, P — QB4
2. Kt — KB3, Kt — QB3 or 2. Kt — QB3, Kt — QB3
3. P — Q4, P x P   3. P — KKt3, P — KKt3
4. Kt x P, Kt — B3   4. B — Kt2, B — Kt2
5. Kt — QB3, P — Q3   5. P — Q3, P — K3

Queen's Pawn Openings

Queen's Gambit

1. P — Q4, P — Q4 or	1. P — Q4, P — Q4
2. P — QB4, P x P	2. P — QB4, P — K3
3. Kt — KB3, Kt — KB3	3. Kt — QB3, Kt — KB3
4. P — K3, P — K3	4. B — Kt5, B — K2
5. B x P, P — B4	5. P — K3, 0 — 0
6. 0 — 0, P — QR3	6. Kt — B3, P — KR3
7. Q — K2, Kt — B3	7. B — R4, Kt — K5

King's Indian Defence

1. P — Q4, Kt — KB3 or
2. P — QB4, P — KKt3
3. Kt — QB3, B — Kt2
4. P — K4, P — Q3
5. Kt — B3, 0 — 0
6. B — K2, QKt — Q2
7. 0 — 0, P — K4

Nimzo-Indian Defence

1. P — Q4, Kt — KB3
2. P — QB4, P — K3
3. Kt — QB3, B — Kt5
4. P — QR3, B x Kt ch.
5. P x B, P — B4
6. P — K3, 0 — 0

The examples given represent openings that are frequently used in chess, but there are, of course, many different variations of each of the systems illustrated and also very many other types of openings altogether. They all represent, however, attempts to carry out the same basic principles of opening play as indicated earlier in this book, and it may be of interest to the beginner to note how these principles are applied in the examples given.

CONCLUSION

This book constitutes a very brief attempt to cover the enormous subject of "How to Play Chess", but if the novice works through the examples carefully with a set and board in front of him he will begin to absorb the fascination of this, the finest indoor game in the world. His course thereafter is clear; to join a chess club and to develop his play by constant practice and the tuition of more experienced members. The main school of chess, however, is experience, and nothing but playing hard and often, will really make a player.

Chess clubs do not always advertise themselves as well as they might, and if the novice does not know where his nearest club is, he should apply to the Secretary whose address is:—

British Chess Federation,

48, Beacontree Avenue,

London, E17.

The Secretaries change as time goes on and full details of chess clubs throughout the country can always be found in the Year Book of the British Chess Federation, copies of which can be obtained through any bookseller or through a public Library.

PROBLEMS (Pawn Endings)

In all problems White plays from bottom of board.

Fig. 1 White to play and win

Fig. 2 White to play and win

Fig. 3 White to play and win

Fig. 4 White to play and Black to win

SOLUTIONS

(1) White wins by 1.K-K5,K-B2; 2.K-B5, K-Q1; 3.K-Kt6,K-B2; 4.K-B7,K-Q1; 5.K-B8,K-B2; 6.KxP and wins.

(2) White gains his objective by moving his king along the lines of a triangle, e.g. 1.K-Q5,K-B1; K-Q4,K-Q1; (if... K-B2 then 3.K-B5 as in the text) 3.K-B4,K-B1; 4.K-Q5—the move which forces Black to give up the opposition —K-B2: (forced otherwise 5.K-Q6 wins) 5.K-B5,K-B1; 6.K-Kt6,K-Kt1; 7.KxP, K-B2; 8.K-Kt5,K-B1; 9.K-Kt6, K-Kt1; 10.P-B7ch, K-B1; 11.P-R6, K-Q2; 12.K-Kt7 wins.

(3) The technique is for the White King to go to the other side when the Black King cannot keep him out, e.g. 1.K-K3,K-K3; 2.K-Q3,K-Q2; 3.K-B3, K-B3; 4.K-Kt4,K-Kt3; 5.K-R4! (this is the point of the manœuvre. Black cannot now oppose the White King by 5...K-R3 because of 6.P-K6! and queening) K-B3; 6.K-R5,K-B2; 7.K-Kt5,K-Q2; 8.K-B5,K-K3; 9.K-B6 and the Black Pawn is now lost.

(4) Here White is in a position to stop the Black Pawn from queening; but he cannot maintain his King in this commanding position, e.g. 1.P-Q4,K-Kt2; 2.P-Q5,K-B2; 3.K-B4 and Black wins by P-R7.